The POWER GUIDE to Supportive Selling

By
Peter K. Bruening

Word Association Publishers

Tarentum, Pennsylvania

The Power Guide To Supportive Selling

ISBN: 978-1-59571-191-5
Library of Congress Control Number: 2007925485

Word Association Publishers
205 Fifth Avenue
Tarentum, Pennsylvania 15084
www.wordassociation.com
1-800-827-7903

I dedicate this book to my family
— Marga, Jaye and Ross.
It is with your love and your incredible support
that I am able to pursue and live my
dreams in life.

I would also like to thank Tom and Stephanie at Word Association
Publishers for your wonderful assistance. Without your help, this
book would still be just a thought in my mind.

<u>CONTENTS</u>

INTRODUCTION

We have entered an exciting new age of selling. And in this new age, those sales and business professionals who fully embrace an approach called Supportive Selling will be the big winners, along with their customers and clients. We have seen the job of selling evolve from one where it was largely about telling and convincing.

Then, in the last quarter of the 20th century, the landscape of selling began to shift. Successful sales people were those who were leveraging a number of new techniques and approaches. A new vocabulary emerged to describe the field of sales. Terms such as Relationship selling, Customer-focused selling, Question-based selling, Consultative selling and 'Soft' selling entered the mainstream of the sales profession. These were new and encouraging developments.

In the 21st century, these approaches have continued to evolve into an approach that fully integrates what was happening in the late 20th century. Selling is no longer about simply focusing on the customer. While this continues to be critically important, the Master Sales Person is able to make a true connection with the customer that goes beyond simply using customer-focused techniques. It is an entirely new way of thinking about sales. It is a new philosophy — and it is called Supportive Selling.

Whether you are brand new to the world of sales, or whether you are a seasoned professional, this book will lead you on a journey into this exciting new world of selling and serving. In the 21st century, those who succeed in sales will be those who are able to make it a fulfilling and enjoyable process for both the customer and the sales person.

If you are reading this introduction for the purpose of deciding whether or not to purchase this book — or even if you are trying to decide whether to invest the time in reading the entire book — allow me to provide some assistance.

If you view selling as something that the salesperson does *to* the prospect—in other words, you believe that selling is a process where the objective of the sales person is to manipulate another person—then this book is going to provide you with a completely different viewpoint. That is not my perspective of what successful selling is.

If, on the other hand, you view selling as something that the salesperson does *with* the prospect—or if you would like to develop that perspective—this book will be right up your alley.

As the title of this book suggests, there is a method of selling that is specifically designed to view the entire sales process as an exercise in supporting the needs of the prospective customer. In my experience of over twenty years in sales, sales management, sales consulting, sales training, sales coaching and public speaking, this single idea has proven to be one of the most refreshing concepts to many of the thousands of sales people and prospective sales people with whom I have had the good fortune to work.

When I started my sales career back in the early 1980's, I had an impression of myself that was completely opposite of what many of us think a sales person is supposed to be. I was uncomfortable with the idea of manipulating another person—and my impression of what the process of 'Closing' entailed was a frightening and highly unappealing thought.

You may rest assured that the inner voice that told me to keep at it—that there was something to this 'sales thing'—was one of the best things that has ever happened to me. I can honestly say that there is not another career in the business world that I would rather be in than sales. And this is coming from a person with an MBA from the University of Pittsburgh—Katz Graduate School of Business. The general expectation of someone with this type of academic background, at least as far as I knew at the time, was to pursue a career in executive management, or something along those lines.

My first position out of graduate school was as a financial analyst for IBM. That was a prototypical position for a young MBA graduate. The truth is that I truly despised the position from the first day I started, and my dislike grew a little bit every day—until after four years, I was absolutely miserable. It was at that point that I took a chance on a career in selling. And the rest is a satisfying personal story of success, fulfillment and happiness.

Quite simply, selling, when it is done from the perspective of helping—of *assisting* and *supporting* your prospective customer—is a tremendously satisfying career. And this includes emotional as well as financial satisfaction.

By the way, before you continue, I suggest that you get a pen, or a highlighter, and mark this book up as you read it. I can tell you that after reading hundreds of books—sales books, biographies of successful people, business books, self-development books, classic literature, etc.—the way to get the most out of reading books is to learn from them. And there are a few things you can do to maximize the learning process as you read.

First, mark the book up as you read it! That's right. Forget about everything you learned from your librarian in grade school. (I'm assuming, of course, that you are the owner of the book you are marking up!) Underline, highlight, circle. Do whatever will allow you to emphasize and remember the points that make an impact on you as you read them. It has been proven that the act of writing activates a different part of your brain than simply reading, and that this will help you to internalize the information you are trying to learn.

The second thing you can do with this type of book is re-read it. This book was designed to be an ongoing reference to be used by the reader for the purpose of developing sales expertise. There are many books in my personal library that I continually re-read, and I learn something new every time.

And finally, take action! Albert Einstein defined insanity as a person doing the same thing over and over, and expecting different results. What he meant was that if you are trying to generate different results—improved sales results and higher earnings, for example—you must first change your actions. So when you see something in this sales book that is not something you are already doing, and it seems like it may work, try it! That is the only way you will learn and improve.

Remember that sales is an honorable profession—without people to do the selling, businesses would fail to exist. Sales is also a skilled craft—it is a science and an art at the same time. Each of us in this profession and craft can strive to be a 'Master Sales Person'. The Master Sales Person is a lifelong student of sales—and one who never stops learning and improving.

Let's get started on our journey into the world of Supportive Selling!

CHAPTER 1

THE SALES PROCESS

Let's start at the very beginning. If you're anything like I am, you probably thought for a long time—or maybe you even still believe this—that some people can just sell, and some people can't. It's the old natural born salesperson argument—I would even call it a myth. I will grant you that some people have some talents and natural gifts that may help them to learn how to sell in a shorter time period than others.

I feel it is an important point to make, however, that I have seen many people succeed in sales that did not fit the generally accepted 'typical' profile of the natural born sales person. You know the type—the extroverted small talker who is comfortable in any social or business situation. And I have also seen many people fail in sales who *did* fit this profile. The only logical conclusion I have been able to reach is that your talents and gifts are just one aspect of your capability to succeed in sales.

So what else is there? What does it really come down to? The first thing is desire and attitude. Without the deep down desire to succeed at sales, or at anything in life for that matter, you simply cannot excel at it. But even with this desire, you are going to need one very basic advantage. This advantage is a repeatable, simple and effective sales process.

I used to think that successful sales people just went out and talked to prospects, and somehow they just knew what to say, how to say it, and when to say it—almost like it was some kind of black magic or something. That was long ago, before I participated as a student in hundreds of hours of sales training, before I taught hundreds of hours of sales training, before I read hundreds of books about sales, and before I made hundreds of thousands of dollars per year for myself in sales commissions!

What I learned was this: Those of us who succeed in sales don't just go out and wing it. We take a proven process into the field every single day, and we execute the steps of this process with proficiency and efficiency. Our *proficiency* is our level of skill. Proficiency results from practicing, doing, failing, learning, improving—and then repeating this process over and over again. Our *efficiency* is our ability to improve over time so that we can do things with the minimal investment of effort. Efficiency results from prioritizing and committing to the basic daily fundamental sales activities—and then following through on this commitment every single day.

The Supportive Selling Process

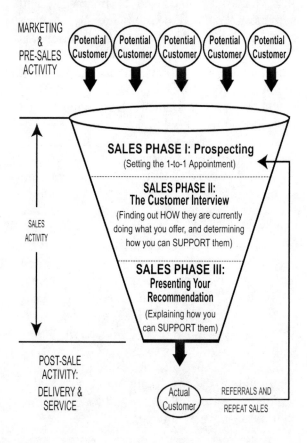

The Supportive Selling Process Can Be Compared To A Funnel

• Marketing and Pre-Sales Activities are those actions that are intended to build awareness among the sales person's target market, and to feed the first phase of selling.

• Sales Activity is broken into three types of actions:
  1. Prospecting is focused on setting 1-to-1 appointments with potential customers.
  2. The Customer Interview is focused on learning about the prospective customer's current situation.
  3. Presenting Your Recommendation is focused on showing the prospective customer how the sales person can assist and support them in improving their current situation.

• Post-Sale Activities are those actions that are intended to provide additional business opportunities in the form of referrals and additional sales to existing customers.

THE SALES PROCESS ...
STARTING WITH MARKETING

There are three core steps to the selling process—which I will refer to as the three Phases of selling. There is also a Pre-sales step that occurs prior to these three sales Phases, and a Post-sales step that occurs after them. While the Pre- and Post-sale steps are actually outside of the core sales process, I prefer to include them in any comprehensive discussion of the overall sales process because they are critically important to the success of any sales professional or business.

The Pre-sales step is called Marketing. Anything that happens prior to your initiation and scheduling of a 1-to-1 discussion with a prospective customer is marketing. Marketing is generally characterized by activities that are designed to reach multiple people at a time, and the purpose of these activities is to create awareness about you, your business, and your products or services.

Examples of marketing activities are plentiful. They include advertising, business networking groups, direct mail or email, newsletters, or any number of other activities, depending upon the market you are trying to reach. Each of these activities is a different way of reaching multiple people in a short period of time to generate awareness. But what these activities don't usually do is actually result in a specific appointment for you to have a 1-to-1 discussion with a prospective customer. In other words, they will rarely if ever, on their own, result in a sale.

SALES PHASE 1:
PROSPECTING

The first Phase in the core sales process, which is often fed by the Marketing step, is called Prospecting. Prospecting is the process of setting up an appointment to have a 1-to-1 discussion with a prospective customer. The purpose of this appointment is to talk about the prospective customer, their business, and eventually, how you may be able to help them—or *support* them—in what they are trying to accomplish. There are various ways to successfully accomplish the Prospecting Phase, and they are discussed in Chapter 3 of this book.

SALES PHASE 2: THE CUSTOMER INTERVIEW

The second Phase in the core sales process, which is the heart of all success in sales, is called The Customer Interview. The importance of executing this Phase well— which includes spending the necessary time in the interview process, and executing it in the proper sequence—cannot be overemphasized. There will not be any consistent or long-term sales success without the development of excellent Customer Interview skills.

This Phase is the process of establishing a dialogue with the prospective customer that effectively does several things. First, it allows you to create rapport with that person. There is an old saying in sales that people buy from people—and I will add to that by saying that, more often than not, they buy from people they like. So, good sales people are excellent at being able to execute The Customer Interview in a way that creates positive rapport with their prospective customers.

As a side note on this issue, I have heard some sales consultants say that it is not important to be liked by your prospective customer—that it is only important to be respected. Don't believe this for a second. Even if you were able to create respect without the person liking you—which is a formidable challenge—there will always be a competitor who will be able to create respect and also be likeable at the same time. Trust me—most things being equal, people buy from people they like. Period.

The second thing The Customer Interview must allow you to do is to gain valuable pieces of information about the prospective customer's situation:

- What are they trying to accomplish?
- How are they currently trying to accomplish it?
- What level of success are they having?
- How was the decision made to pursue their current course of action?
- What reasons might they have for trying something different?

These are just some of the questions that are at the heart of the sales process, because they will eventually become the key elements to the Master Sales Person's recommended proposal. The philosophy of this process is Supportive Selling, which is really what this book is mainly about. During the Customer Interview, the sales person learns exactly what the prospective customer is looking for, and is then able to present a recommended proposal that *supports* both the person and the person's objectives. Many sales people say they are trying to do this, but too few actually do it.

The final outcome of a good Customer Interview is that it leads logically to the next event in the sales process. The ideal next event will be an agreement by the prospective customer to listen to and consider a proposed recommendation by the sales person. (There are other potential next events at the end of a good Customer Interview — such as a follow-on meeting to continue the interview process and gain more information — but the ideal next event, at some point in time, will be to move the process into the Presenting the Recommendation Phase.)

There are some powerful and effective techniques to move through this interview process, and these will be discussed in Chapter 4 of this book.

SALES PHASE 3:
PRESENTING THE RECOMMENDATION

The third Phase in the core sales process—and it must be held off until after an effective Customer Interview has been executed—is Presenting the Recommendation. Too many times, we as sales people want to jump in and present our capabilities too early in the sales process.

If there is a single error that I see committed most often, this is it. To this day, after decades of successful selling, I still fall into this trap occasionally. I get so excited about what I can offer, that I absolutely know I can help my prospective customer. And I jump the gun by not closing out The Customer Interview before moving into my recommendation. This is almost always disastrous in the sales process.

There is another old saying in sales that a person doesn't care how much you know until they know how much you care. A Master

Sales Person will show their prospective customer how much they care during The Customer Interview. This will earn them the right for the customer to care how much they know when they eventually Present the Recommendation.

AFTER THE SALE ...
DELIVERY & SERVICE

Finally, the Post-sale step is Delivery & Service—this is delivering what was sold, and servicing the customer on an ongoing basis. It is estimated, across industries, that it is 5 to 10 times more costly and time consuming to sell to a new customer than to sell additional products or services of similar revenue value to an existing customer. For this reason, it is crucial to successful selling that the follow-through after the sale is done with extreme care and attention.

There are two wonderful things that happen when you ensure good Delivery &

Service. First, your customer becomes a prime opportunity to buy additional products or services from you. And second, they become a great reference and source of referrals for you, thus helping you acquire new customers.

On the other hand, poor Delivery & Service will kill a business and a sales person's career. Dissatisfied customers are the absolute worst thing that can happen to a business, because not only do they stop buying from you, but they also spread the word about their bad experience. It has actually been proven that dissatisfied customers will tell more people—up to ten times as many—about their bad experience with you than satisfied customers will tell about their good experience. It just seems to be human nature to want to spread bad news!

Good sales people pay attention and care to each of these steps:

- Pre-Sale: Marketing
- Sales Phase 1: Prospecting

- Sales Phase 2: The Customer Interview
- Sales Phase 3: Presenting
  the Recommendation
- Post-Sale: Delivery & Service

Now you know *what* you need to do to succeed. That is at least half the battle, because you have a road map to follow. Let's move on to *how* you do it.

CHAPTER 2
THE PRE-SALE: MARKETING

As the diagram on page 20 in Chapter 1 illustrates, we can think about the sales process as a funnel. At the top end of the funnel is the wider end, which is the point of entry into the funnel. And the bottom end is the narrower opening, which is the point of exit from the funnel.

Above the top of the funnel is the marketing process. The purpose of the marketing process is to create prospective customers for your business.

These prospective customers are then 'loaded' into the funnel—which is the sales process. The reason for using the funnel shape as a metaphor is that we know—and this is true for any business of any type—that not every prospective customer will become an actual buying customer. It would be great if every prospective customer became a buying customer, but this is not the case, no matter how effective a sales person may be.

The funnel represents the concept that you must load more prospective customers into the top of the funnel—into the wider end—

with the objective of getting as many as possible to exit the bottom of the funnel — the narrower end — as actual buying customers.

MARKETING & NON-MARKETING ACTIVITIES

Keeping the picture of the funnel in your mind, you can think about the purpose of the Marketing step as providing a constant stream of potential customers to be converted into prospective customers, at which point they are 'officially' loaded into the sales funnel. (The difference between *potential* and *prospective* customers is significant, and will be discussed and clarified in Chapter 3.)

Does every business have a marketing process? The answer is actually 'No'. I have worked with many businesses that locate their prospective customers entirely from non-marketing activities. Most of my clients, however, engage in both marketing and non-marketing pre-sale activities.

There are two main types of non-marketing pre-sale activities that can be used to load the sales funnel. These are cold telephone calls, and cold walk-ins.

The reason these two activities are defined as non-marketing activities is that they are designed to communicate to one person at a time, for the purpose of scheduling a 1-to-1 sales discussion. Remember that marketing activities, on the other hand, are defined as activities that are designed to communicate to multiple people at one time for the purpose of creating awareness about you and your business.

THE DECISION YOU NEED TO MAKE

The differentiation between marketing and non-marketing activities is important. There is a decision you will need to make concerning your approach to loading your sales funnel. Actually, you must choose one of three following alternatives to load your sales funnel:

1. Will you use marketing **and** non-marketing pre-sales activities?
2. Will you use marketing activities only?
3. Will you use non-marketing pre-sales activities only?

Some of you work for large corporations, and you may be tempted to take this section lightly. You are supported by marketing activities that your company provides for you, so you feel that marketing is not something you need to worry about.

While this may be somewhat true, there is also a disadvantage to the fact that these activities are generally beyond your control. They are not designed to specifically help *you* to sell more, but are designed to help the company overall. While these marketing activities may build awareness for your company, I suggest that you also at least consider creating some additional marketing activities that are focused specifically on you, not just on your company.

After all, as a sales person, you are an independent business person—so the more you can control and focus all of your marketing and sales efforts, the more likely these efforts are to drive the specific results you are trying to create.

As you examine each of these questions, keep in mind that you can only answer 'Yes' to one of them. It's important to make a specific choice between the three options, and to know why you are making that choice. This way, if you need to go back and make adjustments in your overall sales process because your sales results are not meeting your expectations, you can review your reasoning behind your marketing decisions. This may lead you to make changes to this part of your sales process.

So let's take a look at the three questions you need to answer for your specific business.

QUESTION #1:
Will you use Both Marketing and Non-Marketing Pre-Sales Activities?

I list this question first, because this is how the majority of businesses, and sales people, go to market. They realize that the need to load the sales funnel can most likely be best served by participating in both marketing and non-marketing pre-sales activities.

If you decide that this is not the correct course for you to follow, then you need to be absolutely sure that by engaging in only marketing—or only non-marketing pre-sales activities—you can generate the number of prospective customers necessary to load into your sales funnel.

SALES GOALS, ACTIVITY TARGETS & SUCCESS RATIOS

The way to help you make this determination is to look at how many end customers you need to generate to meet your goals, then work backward through your sales process to arrive at the number of prospective customers you will need to load into the top of your funnel.

For the purpose of demonstration, let's say that you need to make 10 sales per month to meet your goals. And let's say you know that for every 10 proposal presentations you give, four people buy. This is a 40% success ratio. From this information, we know that:

- Goal = 10 sales per month
- A 40% success ratio at this point in the sales process yields the following requirement:

Proposal Presentations = 25 per month
(40% of your 25 proposal presentations will result in 10 sales.)

Working backward through the process—or upward in the funnel—let's also say that for each 10 prospective customers with whom you begin a conversation, two of them will progress with you to the point of agreeing to listen to your recommended proposal presentation. This is a 20% success ratio. With this information, we now also know that:

- A 20% success ratio at this point in the sales process yields the following requirement:

    Prospective Customers = 125 per month
    (20% of the 125 prospective customers will result in 25 proposal presentations.)

In this example, your simplified sales funnel looks like the following diagram:

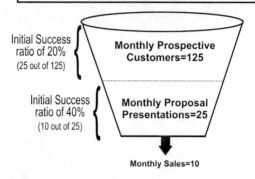

A simplified view of the
Sales Funnel **PRIOR** to improvement

Initial Success
ratio of 20%
(25 out of 125)

**Monthly Prospective
Customers=125**

Initial Success
ratio of 40%
(10 out of 25)

**Monthly Proposal
Presentations=25**

Monthly Sales=10

Let's review how these numbers were determined. If you need 10 sales, and you know that you close four out of 10 recommended proposals, then you need to make 25 proposal presentations. (40% of 25 proposal presentations equals 10 sales—which is your sales goal.)

Now you can move back one additional step in the process. You know you need to generate 25 presentations, and you also know that two out of every 10 prospective customers you begin a conversation with will advance to the proposal stage. If you need to make 25 proposal presentations, then you need 125 prospective customers. (20% of 125 prospective customers equals 25 proposal presentations.)

You must understand a couple of important points about these numbers. First, they can be vastly different by industry. And even within industry, they can differ greatly by company, and among the sales people within that company.

Second, these ratios are not static for any one sales person. As a matter of fact, they should not be static, but should always be improving. One of the main purposes of this sales book is to help you become more **proficient** and more *efficient* in your sales activities. With proficiency you become better at execution, and with efficiency you become faster at execution. Improvements in both of these areas will allow you to improve your personal numbers.

For example, let's take a look at what would happen with some slight improvements to the assumptions in this current example. Let's say you improve your skills and behavior so that you are now able to make five sales instead of four for each 10 proposal presentations—this would be an improvement from a 40% success ratio to a 50% ratio at this point in the sales process.

And let's say that you are also able to increase the number of prospective customers that advance to the proposal presentation stage from only two out of 10 to three out of 10—an improvement from a 20% success ratio to a 30% ratio at this point in the sales process.

With the same monthly goal of 10 sales, your adjusted required monthly sales activity would now look like this:

- Goal = 10 sales per month
- Proposal Presentations = 20 per month   (You have reduced this number by 5)

- Prospective customers = 67 per month (You have reduced this number by 58!)

A simplified view of the Sales Funnel **PRIOR** to improvement

Initial Success ratio of 20% (25 out of 125)

Monthly Prospective Customers=125

Initial Success ratio of 40% (10 out of 25)

Monthly Proposal Presentations=25

Monthly Sales=10

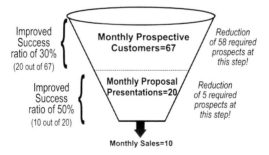

Narrowing the Sales Funnel through Process and Skill improvement

Improved Success ratio of 30% (20 out of 67)

Monthly Prospective Customers=67

Reduction of 58 required prospects at this step!

Improved Success ratio of 50% (10 out of 20)

Monthly Proposal Presentations=20

Reduction of 5 required prospects at this step!

Monthly Sales=10

If the math is not entirely clear to you at this point, don't get too wrapped up in that aspect of the example. You can come back to it at a later time. Just understand that the point of looking at your personal numbers is to fully comprehend a couple of things.

First, even slight improvements at various points in the sales process—the previous example only showed an incremental improvement of 1 at two stages of the sales process—can equate to huge beneficial impacts in terms of how many prospective customers you need to load into your sales funnel.

And the second point is that you must know where your prospective customers are coming from. In either example above—whether you consider the scenario prior to the improvements, or the one after the improvements have been made—the goal of 10 sales per month will not be made unless between 67 and 125 prospective customers are being loaded into the sales funnel each and every month. Prospective customers are the lifeblood of any sales person's livelihood.

And that brings the discussion back around to the first question that must be answered relative to marketing. Are you going to use both marketing and non-marketing pre-sales activities to generate whatever number of prospective customers you need in order to make your goals?

If you don't know, I suggest that you answer this question 'Yes', and that you start with both marketing and non-marketing pre-sales activities for your business. I load the funnel for my sales consulting business by using both of these methods.

For marketing activities, I do a number of things. First, I send out some direct mail, I send out some email, I do a little bit of advertising, and I also do a fairly substantial amount of business networking. These are all important marketing activities for my business.

The topic of business networking is worthy of an entire book, but the one point I will make about business networking is that it is only effective when it is engaged in for the long-term, and when it is viewed as a way to generate warm referrals and warm pre-sales calls.

The whole basis of business networking is that you look for ways to generate referrals for other people in your networking groups. To do this, you introduce them to people in your own personal network who may be able to use their products or services. The universal law of reciprocation will eventually bring referrals back your way.

For non-marketing pre-sales activities, I do one primary activity, and that is cold telephone contacts. I have done cold walk-ins, and I have also trained sales people to do both cold telephone contacts and cold walk-ins. Again, these are being defined as non-marketing activities because they are 1-to-1 methods of communication. But they are also pre-sales, because the person being contacted has not yet agreed to engage in a Customer Interview.

While cold walk-ins can be effective, it is a less efficient process than the telephone. As a general rule, you can reach a lot more people in a shorter period of time using the telephone than you can by doing cold walk-ins. Think about how long it would take to call ten people on the phone, versus walking into ten different businesses. Both of these pre-sales methods will be discussed in more detail in Chapter 3.

Let's say you're not convinced that you need to do both marketing and non-marketing pre-sales activities to generate your necessary prospective customers. If this is the case, then you can move on to the second question.

QUESTION #2:
WILL YOU USE MARKETING ACTIVITIES ONLY?

If you are going to opt for this alternative, please do so with a great deal of caution. It is very tempting to think that you will not have to engage in any cold contact, or even warm contact, pre-sales activity. It is also tempting to believe that by creating the perfect marketing piece, with the perfect message, and the perfect artwork—and then by sending it to the perfect list—prospective customers will beat a path to your door! The bottom line is that this simply will not work for the vast majority of businesses.

If a marketing-only approach is to succeed, then your business will most likely need to fit a certain profile. First, your market is characterized by a high number of people who are in the 'Already Looking' status. This means that, because of the nature of your product, there is a need you fill that is readily apparent to your prospective customers. They do not need or want to engage in a sales discussion with you.

As a result, they are actively looking for products or services such as yours. You simply need to get your message into the marketplace, and you will attract these active buyers. These types of businesses may include restaurants, retail stores or consumer products.

In this type of business, you do not need to motivate people to make a buying decision — because that decision has been made already. What you need to do is to motivate them to make a buying decision for *your* product or service rather than someone else's. Motivating someone to buy, versus motivating someone to choose your product or service when they have already decided to buy on their own, are two entirely different marketing and sales challenges.

The second aspect that will likely characterize your business profile if a marketing-only approach is to succeed is that you will spend more of your budget on your marketing than most companies. As a result, you likely will not have a sales force because all or a majority of your sales and marketing budget will be allocated to marketing activities.

This sales book is not primarily designed for marketing-only businesses. While many of the concepts in the book will apply to marketing-only and consumer businesses, it is primarily designed for companies and professionals who sell to other business customers, as opposed to business-to-consumer markets. Business-to-business selling requires a more focused and active role in the sales process.

The fact is that most of us in the business world serve markets that are not predominantly made up of prospective customers who are in the 'Already Looking' status. The result is that we need to spend more time and effort in the pre-sales activities, because our sales process is going to require more of a personal dialogue and relationship with potential and prospective customers.

While it may seem disadvantageous at first to be involved in this type of business—again, many of us have that temptation to want to avoid sales because it's difficult—it is actually a great ***advantage*** to be in a business that requires this level of active pre-sales and sales activity. The reason is that it gives you, as the sales person, a lot more control over your performance and financial returns—and as a result, more control over your life. It also makes your sales skills very valuable to all types of businesses.

As long as you know your personal numbers, all you need to do is focus on the points of the sales process where you can improve. By doing this, you can determine your own results.

Let's say you're not convinced that you need to do both marketing and non-marketing pre-sales activities to generate your necessary prospective customers, but you also know that marketing alone will not work for you. If this is the case, then you will probably answer 'Yes' to the third question—or you may choose to go back and reconsider the first question.

QUESTION #3:
WILL YOU USE NON-MARKETING
PRE-SALES ACTIVITIES ONLY?

This is certainly a viable alternative, and there are many businesses and professional sales people who opt for this method. There are two primary non-marketing pre-sales activities that are used to load the sales funnel—cold call telephone contacts and cold walk-ins. I use the terms 'cold call' and 'cold walk-in' knowing that they sometimes conjure a negative image in the minds of sales people. I would like to suggest that you do not think of the word 'cold' as either negative or positive, but only as a qualification of the level of prior relationship you have with the person you are contacting. A cold contact is simply a contact with someone who does not know you, and who is not expecting your call.

This, of course, means that there is such a thing as warm calling. Warm calling is much easier for many people to do, and it can be very effective, but it usually requires more advance effort and a longer lead time than cold contacts. This will be explained in more detail in Chapter 3.

Business networking is a great way to generate warm calls. A warm call is simply a contact to someone who does know you—possibly personally, or maybe only by name through a mutual contact—and who may even be expecting your call.

One thing to remember about warm calling versus cold calling is that while your success ratios will generally be higher with warm calls—and I am defining success in this context as being able to generate enough interest during your call to get someone to agree to make an appointment to talk with you face-to-face—there are some people you most likely will not be able to reach without making some cold calls. Either way, superior telephone skills will provide a sales person with a tremendous advantage.

There will be more discussion about the methods of cold and warm calling in Chapter 3.

CHAPTER 3

THE 1ST PHASE OF SELLING: SELLING: PROSPECTING

Prospecting is the point at which the overall sales and marketing process leaves the marketing step, and enters the first of the three core Phases that make up the sales funnel. Until this point, all of the sales person's activities have been designed to create awareness through marketing activities—or they have been designed to create interest through non-marketing pre-sales activities—and to lead to an eventual 1-to-1 sales conversation. Prospecting is the moment of truth when a *potential* customer becomes a *prospective* customer.

POTENTIAL VERSUS PROSPECTIVE CUSTOMERS

The difference between a potential customer and a prospective customer is fairly easy to describe. A potential customer is someone who meets the profile—or the target criteria—of a likely buyer. A potential customer can also be described as a target customer. Marketing and pre-sales activities are directed toward these target customers with the intent of converting as many of them as possible to prospective customers.

A prospective customer differs from a potential customer in that the prospective customer has made a decision to start a sales conversation with the sales person. The prospective customer has agreed to an appointment—or a meeting—to talk with the sales person. And this appointment must exist on the prospective customer's calendar. It is not a vague future event—such as "Give me a call next week"—but is a specifically scheduled event—such as "I'll see you this Wednesday at my office at 2:00". It is a specific calendar event.

This difference is absolutely critical. The sales process has not begun until the Prospecting Phase has been completed. And the Prospecting Phase has not been successfully completed until an appointment has been set with the potential customer. At this point, the potential customer—or target customer—becomes a prospective customer.

SELLING THE APPOINTMENT

Now that you understand that the Prospecting Phase is the conversion of a potential customer to a prospective customer, the actual objective of the Prospecting Phase should become clear. The entire objective of the Prospecting Phase is to set an appointment. Another way I like to describe it is that the objective of this Phase is to actually *sell* the appointment.

At this point in the sales process, you are definitely selling. But you are not selling your product or service. What you *are* selling is an appointment to execute the Customer Interview Phase—which will eventually lead to you actually selling your product or service.

As a matter of fact, the moment you find yourself talking more than just the slightest bit about your product or service, or your company, or yourself, or anything other than why the potential customer should agree to meet with you, you are sacrificing both *proficiency* and *efficiency* in the prospecting process. This will absolutely cost you sales.

Again, I cannot emphasize this too much. Trying to sell too much or too early on the phone places you at a tremendous disadvantage. Unless you are a telephone sales person, and you have no choice but to make your sales presentation over the phone, you should always—repeat *always*—strive to sell only the appointment over the phone.

Good sales people know that they have a much better chance of executing a high quality customer interview, and of making a strong proposal presentation, in person. Body language and eye contact are important selling tools to the Master Sales Person, and they are not present during a phone conversation.

THE IMPORTANCE OF PROSPECTING

Let's take a look at the activities so far that have brought the sales person to this point. Through marketing activities, pre-sales cold contact techniques, or a combination of these activities—such as using business networking to warm up the contacts—the sales person has focused on a set of targets that look like good potential customers.

The sales person has also set an objective for how many of these potential customers must be converted into prospective customers to meet his or her end sales goal. In the example in Chapter 2, we determined that the improved sales person—on a monthly basis—needed to generate 67 prospective customers, in order be able to present 20 proposals, so that 10 sales could be made.

The importance of the Prospecting process should now be very evident. The question to be asked is: How is this sales person going to generate 67 prospective customers? Remember that these numbers are for illustration only. Your numbers could be much different. Perhaps you need 10 prospective customers in your business or perhaps you need 100. Either way, your process is the same—you have personal numbers, and the better you understand them, the more effectively you will be able to improve them.

If you were the sales person in this example, how would you approach the challenge of creating 67 prospective customers per month? One way to view this is as a business capacity problem, similar to a manufacturing plant. The end product that the sales person is producing out of his or her 'sales factory' is customers. The entire process begins with potential target customers as the raw material for the sales manufacturing process. Everything in between the raw material of potential target customers, and the end product of actual buying customers, is Work-in-Process material.

In a factory, material moves from production step to production step as it is processed at each manufacturing stage. The sales process is exactly the same. The Prospecting Phase is the first stage in this process of 'manufacturing' customer sales. In this Phase, the sales person—who is the foreman of the sales factory—must process raw material, which are the potential target customers, into the first stage of Work-in-Process material, which are the prospective customers.

The Sales Factory

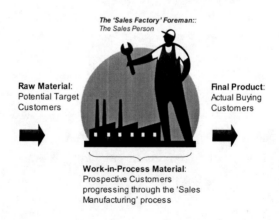

The 'Sales Factory' Foreman::
The Sales Person

Raw Material:
Potential Target
Customers

Final Product:
Actual Buying
Customers

Work-in-Process Material:
Prospective Customers
progressing through the 'Sales
Manufacturing' process

The sales process can be viewed as a 'Sales Factory'.

- Potential Target Customers are the Raw Material that is necessary to feed the process of 'manufacturing' customers.

- As Prospective Customers move through the stages of the Sales Process, they become Work-in-Process material in the 'Sales Factory':
  - As with any manufacturing process, there is waste during each stage. In the 'Sales Factory', this waste is represented by the prospective customers who do not advance to the next stage of the sales process.

- The Final Products of the 'Sales Factory' are Actual Buying Customers.

The success of the 'Sales Factory' is determined by the sales person's ability to efficiently and proficiently input as many potential target customers into the Raw Material stage, move them through the various Work-in-Process stages, and ultimately to the Final Product stage.

How to Make a Good Appointment-Setting Telephone Call

The following script outlines the approach I use to make a good telephone contact for the purpose of scheduling a meeting. It is simple, it is repeatable, and it is effective. And it has one single objective: It is specifically designed to sell appointments. I am in the business of delivering speaking, consulting, training and coaching services in the field of sales & leadership. But when I make an initial phone call, I want to talk as little about those topics as I possibly can. I just want to create enough interest that the person will meet with me.

By the way, if you decide to engage in cold walk-ins, your objective should not generally be to get the decision maker to meet with you at that point in time for a Customer Interview. This may happen in rare cases, but your objective should be to get the name of the person with whom you would like to meet at a future time. Then, when you call back on the telephone, you can use the name of the person you spoke to during your walk-in, and you are making a warmer call.

This same approach can also be used on the phone—you can use an initial phone call to warm up a second call. The way to do this is to ask the person who answers the phone if they might be able to help you out—most people are willing to help someone who asks, and who is making themselves vulnerable by asking for assistance.

For example, tell the person that you have some information that you'd like to mail out to the decision maker—and you wondered if he or she would help out by giving you that person's contact information. Most people will do this for you, because your request for an address to mail information is non-threatening and is easy for them to fulfill. You are much more likely to encounter resistance if you ask that person to put your call through to the decision maker.

Then if you like, you can follow-through by sending an introductory letter to the contact. Do this with the knowledge that there is a very good chance that the letter will not be read or remembered. It actually doesn't matter either way. You are simply following through on what you said you were going to do, which is send a letter to the decision maker.

Then, when you call back the following week or so, you know who to ask for, and you have a reason for calling. This is a good way to warm up prospecting calls. Many sales people feel more comfortable with this approach, and that level of comfort can often help to create a more positive environment for a successful call because of the confidence that results.

I mentioned the word 'script' earlier, and while this is an uncomfortable topic for some sales people, I suggest that you view the phone calling script as an invaluable training tool. It is not something you should read during the prospecting process, any more than a professional football player takes his playbook out on the field of play during a game.

He uses the playbook as a training tool — he uses it to practice and study, and to create new habits, thought patterns and behaviors — so that when he does get out on the field of play, these desired habits, thoughts and behaviors are natural.

The prospecting script is the same thing to the sales person that the playbook is to the professional football player. It is a training tool so that your desired selling behaviors — as well as your thought patterns and habits — become natural and reflexive when you are in the field of selling.

Let's get back to my telephone prospecting approach. I use this basic approach almost every day — the only time I don't use it is when I'm in a client engagement that day, and I can't prospect because of scheduling reasons. Otherwise, I highly suggest that you engage in prospecting every day — or at least as regularly as you possibly can.

Think about it this way: You cannot cram a month's worth of prospecting into the last few days of the month, any more than a farmer can cram a season's worth of planting and fertilizing into the last few days before the harvest. It just won't work. It takes time to 'grow' a healthy sales funnel.

I use the scripts in this book to sell my consulting and speaking services. But these are also the base scripts I customize when I create a training workshop for a client. As you read my scripts, do it with the intent of adjusting them to your business. They are straightforward, and they are being used by thousands of sales people.

My telephone prospecting script follows. (I have used the abbreviations 'SP' to indicate sales person and 'PC' to indicate 'potential customer')

The phone call begins with my introduction and invitation to meet:

SP   "Hello *customer name,* this is Peter Bruening with The SellingPoints Group. Are you familiar with SellingPoints?"

PC   "Yes" or "No"

SP   "Then you probably know ..." (I use this lead-in only if they answer 'Yes' to my initial question. Otherwise I move directly into the following statement.)

"We're a sales consulting firm, and our clients hire us to help them increase their sales, and to shorten their sales cycles. We do this with a combination of consulting, training and coaching services.

The reason I'm calling you, *customer name,* is that I wanted to

> set up some time to talk with you
> about what some of our clients are
> doing—to see if some of these
> things may apply to you.
>
> I was looking at this Wednesday
> morning. How would that be
> for you?"

What would the potential customer say at this point? They can only agree or disagree. There is no other option. If they agree, great! I've converted them from a potential customer to a prospective customer—I simply agree on the specific time, and I now have a calendar event scheduled to move on to the next Phase in the sales process.

And believe it or not, if you make enough of these calls on a regular basis, people will agree to see you after this initial opening. However, what happens when they do not agree?

WHAT TO SAY WHEN THEY
DON'T WANT TO MEET WITH YOU

There are many good sales books that provide techniques on handling sales resistance—or objections, as they are most frequently called. The best advice I can give you is to make this an area of ongoing learning for yourself. The more calls you make, and the more types of 'No's' you hear, the better your instincts and techniques will get for anticipating and answering them.

That being said, there are some basic concrete principles I can offer you to handle most types of sales resistance. First, 'Mail or email me some information' and 'You caught me at a bad time' are not real objections. I call them smokescreen objections, and they are easily dealt with.

This is how I recommend that you handle each of these responses—and I can tell you from proven experience that these approaches will work:

SP   "I was looking at this Wednesday morning. How would that be for you?"

PC   "Why don't you mail me some information … I'll take a look at it and I'll give you a call back after I read it."

SP   "I really appreciate your interest! You know, I call a lot of people, and some have asked me for some information. But they've found it to be a lot more effective for them if we just get together … and then I can leave something behind that's a lot more specific for them.

How is that Wednesday morning?"

There are many reasons why this response works. It thanks the other person, it is 'soft', and it provides a good alternative to their request.

Just believe me—it works. I don't always get the appointment at this point, but I get them off of the desire for me to mail something out, which is almost always a waste of the sales person's time anyway. When you mail information out, it is rarely read by the customer.

Let's take a look at the other smokescreen objection.

SP   "I was looking at this Wednesday morning. How would that be for you?"

PC   "You know, you caught me at a bad time. I was just heading out for a meeting ..."

SP   "That's OK. I figured you were busy right now. I was really calling just to set up a time that would be good.

How is that Wednesday morning?"

It has some similar elements to the prior technique. It acknowledges and respects what the other person said, and it is soft. Once again, it just works. As with the response to 'Mail or email me some information', it may not get me the appointment, but it gets them from trying to rush me off the phone.

If I don't get the appointment when I make these responses, I will usually get their real objection, which is what I want anyway.

There is only one real objection that anyone can have for not wanting to meet with me: They feel that they are already doing OK with another supplier of my service, or that they are already doing OK by not using any supplier of my service. (By the way, if they are doing their sales training internally, I view this as simply using another supplier.) Either way, I want them to tell me this so that I can respond to it.

Let me make that point again. I *want* them to tell me that they don't think they need me, and why, because that allows me to specifically respond to them.

This is how it works:

SP   "I was looking at this Wednesday morning. How would that be for you?"

PC   "You know, I think we're all set with our sales training. We have a company we work with that does a good job."

SP   "That's great! I figured you were working with someone already. Actually, that's one of the reasons I called. Most of our clients were working with other sales consultants when we called, and a lot of the time we've been able to work in combination with what they were doing.

I'd still like to suggest that it may make sense to get together.

How is that Wednesday
morning?"

It shows respect, it is logical, it is soft, and
it works.

And finally, suppose they don't tell me that
they are already working with someone, but
they just don't want to meet.

This is how this one works:

SP "I was looking at this Wednesday
morning. How would that be for
you?"

PC "You know, I don't think that's
something we're really looking at
right now."

SP "That's not a problem. I talk with
a lot of people, and sometimes the
timing just isn't right.

> A lot of our clients were in a similar situation when I first called, and fortunately we were able to get together, just so I could let them know some of the things that were available, in case they were interested in the future.
>
> I'd still like to suggest that it may make sense to get together.
>
> How is that Wednesday morning?"

I deliver a full workshop on this topic, and I will certainly admit that there are more nuances and techniques than I've been able to cover here. And the live workshop setting is more effective in teaching these techniques.

But you can make quite a positive impact on your sales performance if you can master the above introduction and invitation to meet, and also the ways to handle resistance when you ask for the appointment. Master these techniques as they have been presented here, and build your appointment setting efforts on this foundation and watch your sales funnel grow!

By spending some time customizing these approaches to your business, and then practicing and implementing them, you can quickly find yourself in the 20% of all sales people who set 80% of the appointments and who make 80% of the sales.

The Two Most Common Paths of a Successful Prospecting Phase

The 3 Steps of Appointment Setting

1-Introduction   Call the Potential Target Customer; Deliver an Introduction & Invitation to Meet

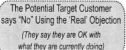

2-Handling Resistance

The Potential Target Customer says "No" Using the 'Real' Objection	The Potential Target Customer says "No" Using a Smokescreen Objection
(They say they are OK with what they are currently doing)	*(They say they are too busy or they request that you mail information)*

| Agree & Affirm; Then suggest that others have used your products or services in combination with what they were currently doing. | Address the Smokescreen Objection Use the appropriate technique, depending on their objection: 1-They are too busy 2-They request you to mail them information |

3-Re-Invitation & Close

Re-Invite the Potential Target Customer to Meet

The Potential Target Customer says "Yes" Confirm the appointment time and hang up

CHAPTER 4

THE 2ND PHASE OF SELLING: THE CUSTOMER INTERVIEW

This chapter is the center-beam of the book. The title of the book refers to a style of selling called 'Supportive Selling'. Up to this point, I have only briefly defined what is meant by this phrase.

WHAT IS SUPPORTIVE SELLING?

In defining what Supportive Selling is, it is useful to compare it to other styles of selling. Supportive Selling is something that the sales person does *with* the prospective customer—not something the sales person does *to* the prospective customer. During the Supportive Selling process, the feeling that the prospective customer gets from the sales person is 'This person is trying to help me'—the prospective customer does not get the feeling that 'This person is trying to sell me something'.

Supportive Selling is based on providing assistance. When you are engaged in Supportive Selling, you are engaged in the process of *serving*. The supportive sales person views the job of selling as synonymous with the job of serving. Supportive sales is actually service.

Before you read further about the Customer Interview Phase of the sales process, it is critically important that you fully immerse your thoughts into a service mentality. When I first began my sales career, my perceptions were very different than they are now—and as a result, I was a much less effective sales person than I am now.

In those days, I thought I had to manipulate the prospective customer to my way of thinking. I thought the key to sales was in my ability to knock down someone's objections one-by-one, and to smooth-talk someone into seeing the advantage that my features would provide for them. And then I would deliver a brilliant presentation that would knock their socks off—and they would simply *have* to buy from me!

I was not good at selling. In truth, I was very bad at selling.

In my business as a sales consultant and trainer, I continue to see sales and business people with this perception of sales every single day. This model of sales is extremely limiting, both to the sales person and to the prospective customer. Neither gets what they want from this type of exchange.

The prospective customer does not receive the benefit of a relationship with a sales person who truly understands what he or she wants and needs. And the sales person does not receive the level of financial or emotional fulfillment that can result from delivering truly supportive sales and service.

For some readers, this concept of Supportive Selling may be quite familiar. The evolution of professional sales has been moving in this direction over the past couple of decades. For other readers this concept may be somewhat new and different.

Either way, I ask you to create a mindset, before continuing with this section, that selling is the same as serving—that selling is asking questions and listening, not talking and presenting—that selling is understanding and assisting, not proposing better & faster features, and cheaper prices, than the competition. Selling is helping—it is assisting someone to accomplish something. The sales process *is* the Customer Interview—and the sales proposal is simply a *response* to this sales process.

THE POWER OF THE CUSTOMER INTERVIEW

What comes to your mind when you think of the word 'Interview'? For most people, the word 'question' comes to mind. Some of the people who interview others for a living are news reporters and talk-show hosts. We are all very familiar with what they do. They ask questions, and they listen. And in the process, they are able to skillfully guide a conversation so that meaningful information is disclosed.

That is exactly what a Master Sales Person does. Imagine a sales person who guides the conversation with a prospective customer—using questions and the art of listening—for the purpose of disclosing useful and meaningful information. This information is what will be used to create a recommended proposal that is uniquely tailored to that specific prospective customer's needs.

Now imagine a sales person who instead uses the opposite approach. Rather than spending the time and effort to interview the prospective customer, the sales person asks some cursory questions and quickly moves into 'presentation mode'. At this point, the prospective customer receives a 'one-size-fits-all' proposal that is focused on the great list of features that the sales person's product or service has—and how cheap they are versus the competition.

Put yourself in the prospective customer's place. Who would you buy from? The first sales person spent the majority of time asking you about your situation, listened to what you said, and then customized a recommendation to your needs.

The second sales person took the more traditional approach, and jumped right into a sales pitch that demonstrated how much they knew about their product or service—but it also demonstrated how little they knew, or cared, about *you*!

I don't know about you, but I would buy from the first sales person. Let's take a closer look at how this Master Sales Person sells.

THE FOUR STEPS OF AN EFFECTIVE CUSTOMER INTERVIEW

There are four essential steps to a good customer interview. Each of these must be executed, and they must be executed in this order:

- Preset the Close / Brief Introduction
- Build Personal Rapport
- Gather Business Information
- Close for the Next Calendar Event

I will describe each step, including its purpose and some examples of scripting and transitional statements for each. The scripts are presented as illustrations, and can also be used as training tools to learn the Supportive Selling method.

Before I do that, however, I'd like to further define 'sales resistance'. This is a very important concept in relation to Supportive Selling. In fact, one of the main reasons that Supportive Selling works is that it is designed to create and maintain a low level of sales resistance throughout the sales process.

WHAT IS SALES RESISTANCE?

Sales resistance is the degree to which the prospective customer feels that he or she is being 'sold'. People have a natural resistance to sales people. Think about experiences you may have had—perhaps while you were purchasing a car, or a house, or any number of products and services. All of us know the feeling of sales resistance. It is a feeling of being put under pressure by a sales person, and different people react to it in different ways—none of which is particularly pleasant. Is that the way you want to make your prospective customers feel? Of course it isn't!

There is another old saying that people hate to be sold, but they love to buy. What this means is that as long as they are in control—as long as they feel that they are making the decision and that they are doing the buying—they are comfortable. But as soon as they feel that they are being sold—that something is being done *to* them, and that they are no longer in control— their resistance to buying increases.

Sales resistance is deadly to successful selling. It can occur at almost any point in the sales cycle—from the Prospecting Phase through to Presenting the Recommendation. But it is particularly likely to occur if the interview is not executed properly.

There are two key points to executing an interview properly. First, it must be the center-beam of the sales process. This means that the Customer Interview is where the sales person must spend most of his or her time during the sales process—and this time must be spent properly.

Second, the four steps of the interview must be patiently completed prior to making any recommendation or proposal to the prospective customer. If there is one single thing that kills most sales, it is presenting a proposal too early! 'Too early' simply means prior to completing a thorough Customer Interview.

CUSTOMER INTERVIEW STEP 1: PRESET THE CLOSE / BRIEF INTRODUCTION

The first step of the Customer Interview is a very quick step and consists of a statement or two by the sales person, followed by a brief description of how the sales person is able to help people. The purpose of the initial statement is to provide a low-pressure introduction to the interview.

When it is executed correctly, this step accomplishes several things. First, it reduces any pre-existing sales resistance to the lowest level possible, because it hands some control over to the prospective customer.

Second, it lets the customer know that at the end of the meeting, the sales person will be asking the prospective customer what he or she thinks should be the next logical step in the process. This will ease the transition into the fourth step of the interview, when it will be time to Close for the Next Calendar Event.

The Preset statement that I like to use is the following:

SP   "I really appreciate the opportunity to meet, and to share some of the things we're doing with our customers.

Right up front, I'll tell you that we aren't always able to help everyone ... but I'll try to give you all of the information you need so that at the end of our meeting, you can decide where we go from there."

This statement is slightly more than 60 words long. Yet it has allowed me to accomplish so much.

First, notice that I don't say that I'm going to *tell* the prospective customer how I can help him or her. That is a sure way to raise the sales resistance level. Instead, I casually mention that I'm going to *share* some of the things we're doing with our other customers. This third party reference is much less threatening than if I immediately start focusing on what I perceive to be the prospective customer's needs. I have not earned the right to make a sales proposal yet.

Next, I openly admit that I may or may not be able to help the prospective customer. Again, this keeps the sales resistance low. The other thing it does is introduces the concept of 'help' into the discussion. By hearing this word, the prospective customer begins to understand that I am coming from a position of wanting to assist.

Next, I state that I consider my role in this discussion to be that of a provider of information—and the role of the prospective customer is to use this information so that he or she can make the decision as to where the process leads from there.

Finally, this statement also presets my close, as you will see later in the chapter when I explain the Close for the Next Calendar Event step. By handing over the decision control to the prospective customer, I essentially establish my right to ask for his or her decision when we get to the end of the meeting.

The wrap-up to this first step is the Brief Introduction. After I have made the above Preset the Close statement, I ask a very easy question for the prospective customer to answer:

SP   "Before we get started, would it
        make sense if I told you a little
        more about what we do?"

This statement does a few things. It is the
first time that I've asked the prospective
customer a question, so it starts to get them
involved by having them provide an answer. It
also gives them an easy question to answer
'Yes' to. Finally, it fulfills a logical
expectation that I, as the sales person, am
going to tell them about what I offer.

The key is, though, that my Brief
Introduction is going to be just that—*brief*.
Remember in Chapter 3 when I discussed my
telephone approach for selling the
appointment? Well I basically take the same
brief introduction of how I help people from
that telephone approach and I use it here:

SP   "We're a sales consulting firm,
        and our clients hire us to help
        them increase their sales, and to

shorten their sales cycles. We do this with a combination of consulting, training and coaching services."

The only thing I may add to this is a specific customer example with which my prospective customer will likely identify. I always try to have one of these ready when I am preparing for a Customer Interview meeting. For example, if this is a bank I'm calling on, I may add something like the following to the above statement:

"For example, we recently completed a program with a bank, similar in size to your bank. They were struggling with customer attrition, and a lack of deposit growth. Their deposits have increased about 25% since we finished the program, and attrition is down about 15%."

This is just one place where good sales examples and stories can be used. All Master Sales People collect stories about how they have been able to help other customers. The most powerful way to show a prospective customer what your capabilities are is to refer to an actual story about how you or your company have helped another customer. This type of story is a proof of your capabilities.

Another one of my favorite old sayings about sales is that 'Selling is Storytelling'. I believe this to be very true. People will remember your sales stories long after your meeting has ended. A good sales story communicates both a "Before" and an "After" picture—how was your customer struggling before they brought you in, and how has their situation improved as a result of working with you?

So if we put the entire script together for the Preset the Close / Brief Introduction Phase, this is how it looks:

SP   "I really appreciate the opportunity to meet, and to share some of the things we're doing with our customers.

       Right up front, I'll tell you that we aren't always able to help everyone … but I'll try to give you all of the information you need so that at the end of our meeting, you can decide where we go from there."

       "Before we get started, would it make sense if I told you a little about what we do?"

PC   "Sure." (You will get this type of answer almost every single time.)

SP   "We're a sales consulting firm, and our clients hire us to help them increase their sales, and to shorten their sales cycles. We do this with a combination of consulting, training and coaching services."

"For example, we recently completed a program with a bank, similar in size to your bank. They were struggling with customer attrition, and a lack of deposit growth. Their deposits have increased about 25% since we finished the program, and attrition is down about 15%."

That's it for the first step of the interview. As you learn how to deliver this naturally, and with confidence, you will start to see that your meetings are starting out much more comfortably. This introduction leads very naturally into the next step.

CUSTOMER INTERVIEW STEP 2: BUILD PERSONAL RAPPORT

The second step of the Customer Interview will vary depending upon the communication style and personality type of the prospective customer, as well as the situation and environment in which the interview is taking place.

When this step is executed correctly, it accomplishes one very important thing: The prospective customer feels that the person he or she is talking with — the sales person — has a true and personal interest in them as an individual. This is the central theme behind building an interpersonal relationship. For any relationship to be created, there must first be interpersonal interest. It is the sales person's job to express this interest.

The concept of 'relationship selling' is certainly not new. There have been many books and training programs created about relationship selling — and this is a valid concept. While Supportive Selling encompasses a much wider range of concepts and techniques, relationship selling is an integral component of the Supportive Selling method.

In my training workshops, I always advise that the sales person should set a goal of asking at least three personal rapport-building questions. With some prospective customers, this will be difficult—sometimes the Build Personal Rapport step may be very short. This usually happens with prospective customers who are less expressive—sometimes called 'Driver/Directors' and 'Thinker/Analyzers' in terms of their communication style.

With other prospective customers, this stage may be very natural, and the Build Personal Rapport step may flow easily and go on for 15 minutes or more. This usually happens with prospective customers who tend to communicate in a more expressive manner—sometimes called 'Relater/Listeners' and 'Socializer/Performers'.

There is a great deal more depth to the topic of communication styles. A sales person can actually read the communication style of the prospective customer, and can then adapt his or her own style to most effectively complement the prospective customer's style. This is an entire training subject in itself, and it is an important ability of the highest performing sales people.

For the purposes of this book, it is enough for the reader to know that it is not necessarily good or bad if the prospective customer happens to be expressive and talkative during this part of the conversation, or if he or she tends to be more closed. Either way, something very important is accomplished by showing personal interest in the prospective customer and making a real effort to build rapport. By making this part of every Customer Interview, you will set yourself apart from at least 80% of all sales people. The vast majority of sales people want to rush as quickly as possible into their presentation. You will be in the 20% who show actual interest in your prospective customer.

The transition statement that I like to use between the Preset the Close/Brief Introduction step and the Build Personal Rapport step is this:

> SP   "I'm curious, how long have you been at XYZ Company?"

That's pretty simple, right? From here I will follow their answer with additional appropriate questions. For example, let's say the prospective customer tells me that they have been at XYZ Company for 10 years. I might follow up with, "Wow, that's great. What other departments have you worked in?" Let's say, instead, that they tell me they have been with XYZ for 1 year. In that case, I might follow up with, "That's great. Where were you prior to XYZ?"

This takes some practice, but when you get in the habit of executing a Build Personal Rapport step in every interview, you will find that, as with any other sales skill, it will become more natural and comfortable for you.

The key to becoming a good interviewer is to show natural curiosity. If you were in a conversation with a friend or neighbor, and they mentioned something that had just hapened—for example, a job change—you would naturally ask them questions. Why did they change jobs? Do they like the new job? Was it closer to home than their old job? Did they like the people there? Etc.

This is exactly what the Master Sales Person does with a prospective customer. They show a natural interest and curiosity in that individual *as a person.*

Some good examples of the types of questions that you can ask during this step of the interview are:

- "So, how long have you lived in this area?"
- "So, what kinds of things do you like to do outside of work?"
- "That's an interesting photo on the wall. Did you take that?"
- Etc, etc, etc.

And you can go on from there. Just remember that this step works very well if your first question is good, which is why I like to ask them how long they've worked at their present company. Their answer is going to give me many other options as far as additional questions I can ask them.

The other thing to realize is that each of the questions in this stage—and you'll see this in the examples I've presented—has the word 'you' in it. These are questions about the prospective customer—they are not about the company, and they are not about the company's objectives. Actually, I try to stay away from the prospective customer's work-related objectives at this point. I want to save those questions for the next step, when I begin to gather business-related information.

Again, think about this step the way you would think about any conversation where you first meet someone, and you want to get to know them a little bit. You would show natural curiosity and interest. As long as you are asking 'you-centered' questions, and you are staying away from doing too much of the talking yourself, you're probably doing a good job of building some rapport.

That's it for the second step of the interview. As you learn how to engage in this back and forth question & answer dialogue naturally and comfortably, you will find a couple of things. First, you will actually learn some things about your prospective customers that you would not have known otherwise—because you will be creating an interpersonal relationship. And second, you'll see a loosening up of the sales environment that will help you lead very naturally into the next step.

CUSTOMER INTERVIEW STEP 3: GATHER BUSINESS INFORMATION

The third step of the Customer Interview is the heart of the interview. During this stage you will gather the information that you really need in order to put together a recommendation that your prospective customer will want to buy.

When everything is said and done, there are two very critical types of information that you need to obtain in this step of the interview:

1. How is the prospective customer already doing what you offer? And how effectively is it working?

2. What reasons would they have to change what they are currently doing?

Let's face it. If you could simply call potential target customers on the phone all day and ask them these few simple questions, and get straightforward and honest answers, selling would be the easiest thing in the world. Think about it. I'd be able to call someone up and say, "How do you currently train your sales force?" They would answer honestly and in a straightforward manner. Then I'd ask, "And how is that working?" Again, they answer in an honest and straightforward manner. Finally I would ask, "What reasons would you have to change how you're currently training your sales force?" And again, I would receive an honest and straightforward answer.

At this point, I would know exactly what my competition is within that account, and I would know what I had to do to either replace them or coexist with them in the account. That's easy!

As we all know, it isn't that easy. And the reason it isn't that easy is that we have to warm up the dialogue before we can get to those critical questions—we have to *earn* the right to be able to ask for that information. That is really what sales is all about.

In actuality, all of us in the sales profession should be very glad that it is not as straightforward as asking those few simple questions. If it was, then there would be virtually no reason for companies to pay the kinds of salaries and commissions that Master Sales People earn, because it would be an incredibly easy job. Anyone could do it.

This is why you are reading this book. This is why you are trying to acquire new habits and techniques. This is why you are learning and growing in the field of sales. And as long as you do this, you will stand out and be in the 20% of the sales profession that earns 80% of the money.

The transition statement that I like to use between the Build Personal Rapport step and the Gather Business Information step is this:

SP   "I was wondering... What experiences have you had with sales training companies in the past?"

Let me be clear on something here. This is always the question I use at this point in the interview—100% of the time. I have experimented with many lead-off inquires to begin asking my business-related questions, and this one is simply the best. There are two reasons it is the best.

First, it is completely open ended. The prospective customer is free to answer this question with whatever comes to mind when I ask this question. And this is exactly what I want. I really want to know what experiences they've had with sales training companies — either positive or negative — or even if they've had no experience at all.

The second reason it is a very good question is that it asks about the past. Questions about the past are easy for someone to answer. As initial questions, they are more comfortable, and less threatening and presumptive to the prospective customer, than asking about what they are currently doing, or about their future plans. Remember that Supportive Selling is built around keeping the level of sales resistance low.

Think about it this way. Imagine that the sales person immediately asks the prospective customer what he or she is currently doing to solve the type of problem that the sales person's company can also solve, rather than starting by asking a much softer question about their past experiences. The prospective customer will have an inner expectation that the sales person is going to launch into all the reasons that his or her company can do it better, faster, cheaper— or something along those lines.

The prospective customer thinks that the sales person is going to say that because they are *conditioned* that way. They have been called on by so many typical sales people who have done exactly that. As a result, they dodge the question —the sales person doesn't get honest information, and the level of sales resistance has been raised. And another sales opportunity is lost.

On the other hand, when you casually ask an open ended question about past experiences—using the specific word 'experiences'—you are making a very natural move from the Building Personal Rapport step. Try this for yourself, and you will be thrilled with the results you get. This question is one of my favorite parts of the entire interview.

It is difficult to script out what specifically happens after this question, because there are many answers that the prospective customer may give. But as with the first question in the Build Personal Rapport step, you will get better at asking natural follow-up questions the more you do this.

As you stay in this area of the prospective customer's past experiences, you are going to learn a few things. First, if they have had experiences with companies in your industry, you will find out if they were positive or negative. Another thing you will likely find out, without even directly asking, is what they are currently doing.

Once a prospective customer tells me what they have done in the past with sales training companies, I will ask questions to get them talking more about what they were able to accomplish with those companies. I always ask them first what they *have* been able to accomplish, not what they were not able to accomplish, because I don't want them to be defensive—again, it's all about low sales resistance. In the process, I usually will also uncover their bad experiences, and the discussion will inevitably migrate to what types of sales training they are currently doing.

This will happen every time, as long as you get the prospective customer to keep talking about past experiences. The discussion will lead to what they are currently doing—or at the very least, it will leave an easy opening to nudge the conversation that way, with a statement like the following:

> SP   "So based on all of those experiences, what kinds of things are you doing now to train your sales people?"

Once again, by showing interest and asking good questions, I have earned the right to ask this question. I didn't just open the meeting with this kind of a frontal probe, but I worked up to it. At this point, I let them talk about what they're doing, and I continue to ask logical follow-on questions to their statements.

Notice here what the Master Sales Person does not do. This is not the time to talk about what you offer, even if the prospective customer states a point of dissatisfaction with his or her current supplier, and you *know* you can do better. Do *not* present your solution now. Instead, the Master Sales Person makes a note of this point, and uses it for full impact when it is time to Present the Recommendation.

This is the time for the sales person to ask questions, and for the prospective customer to talk. The time will come for the sales person to talk and for the prospective customer to listen—but now is not that time.

Now let's discuss how we move the interview from what the prospective customer's past and current experiences are with companies like yours to the key

information you are looking for: What
reasons would they have to change what they
are doing?

Since we know the approach of asking
about past experiences works so well, the idea
is to keep the approach simple and use this
same technique again. At this point, I will ask
this question:

> SP   "In the past, when you've brought
>   in a new sales training company,
>   or a new sales training approach,
>   I'm curious…what were some of
>   the reasons?"

Until you've tried the Supportive Selling
interview the way I've described it here, it is
difficult to understand the power of this
question when it is properly positioned in the
interview. This is often a magically effective
question.

At this point, the prospective customer will
again talk about what he or she has done in

the past, and the conversation will migrate to what they are doing in the present. Except in this case, when they start talking about the present, they are talking about what reasons they would have for making a change *now*!

What they are doing is telling you what you need to propose to them to get their business. Which way of selling do you think is a more effective? Should you have a comfortable discussion with the prospective customer that leads to them telling you what to propose to them in order to get their business? Or should you go in and throw every feature you have at them in the hopes that something appeals to them and they buy from you?

I'll let you make that decision for yourself, but for me, I've learned that the former—which is the Supportive Selling method—is the much more effective style. Not only is the latter method less effective, but it is also less enjoyable for both the sales person and the prospective customer. Trust me—I know because I used to do it.

So if we put the question flow together for the Gain Business Information step, this is how it looks:

SP   "I was wondering... What experiences have you had with sales training companies in the past?"

PC   *Discussion: They will talk about what they've done in the past, and the discussion will either lead to what they are doing now, or you can nudge it that way with a statement like the following:*

SP   "So based on all of those experiences, what kinds of things are you doing now to train your sales people?"

PC   *Discussion: They will talk about what they are currently doing.*

SP   "In the past, when you've brought
        in a new sales training company,
        or a new sales training approach,
        I'm curious…what were some of
        the reasons?"

PC   *Discussion: Again, they will talk
        about what they've done in the
        past, and this time the discussion
        will either lead to what they'd
        like to accomplish now that they
        are not accomplishing, or what
        they would like to accomplish in
        the future.*

I've used sales training as my example,
because this is one of the services I offer. But
I have adapted this approach to a variety of
companies in over 50 industries. It is
completely versatile, and will work for any
product or service. Go ahead and script it out
for your business—that's the first step to
learning how to use it.

That's it for the third step of the interview. During this step, the sales person has gained the real information that will be used to put together a recommended proposal that is tailored to this specific prospective customer. At this point, the sales person knows what the prospective customer is trying to accomplish, and what reasons he or she may have to either replace what they're doing, or to add to it with additional products or services.

But before the sales person presents that recommendation, there is one final step to complete the Customer Interview Phase.

CUSTOMER INTERVIEW STEP 4: CLOSE FOR THE NEXT CALENDAR EVENT

The fourth step of the Customer Interview is to Close for the Next Calendar Event. There are different types of sales cycles in different businesses. In some industries, the sales person may be able to move into making a proposal in the same meeting as the interview. In other industries, the sales person will need to go back to the office with the information that has been gathered during the interview, assemble a proposal, and come back in a follow-up meeting to present it. I will address both of these scenarios.

The statement I use to wrap up the Customer Interview Phase is the following:

SP   "I really appreciate all of the time you've spent with me.

When we first started talking, I told you that you'd be the one to decide where we go from here.

I can tell you that I do have some ideas, based on the information you've given me. And I'd like to show them to you.

Does that make sense?"

Notice that I tie back to the Preset the

Close from the beginning of the interview. I am acknowledging that the decision-making power is in the prospective customer's hands, and I actually am asking permission to present my ideas. If you have had a good discussion with the prospective customer, you will almost always get agreement at this point. (This statement is more of a courtesy, which the prospective customer will appreciate. It is just one more technique that will keep the level of sales resistance low).

We are talking about sales, however, and the reason a funnel shape is used to represent the sales process is that you may not advance every prospective customer to the proposal stage from here. I very rarely have someone decline to see my recommended proposal at this point. By mastering this interview process you will absolutely maximize your personal success numbers.

There is one final, and very important, point concerning the closing of the Customer Interview Phase. If the sales person is able to continue on in the same meeting with the proposal — in other words, no additional work must be done back at the office to prepare the proposal—then he or she can advance directly to the next Phase, which is Presenting the Recommendation.

If, however, the sales person does need to come back for a future meeting to present the proposal, he or she must—and this is an absolute *must*—do everything possible to set a specific calendar event to do so. This does not mean that the sales person says to the customer, 'I'll call you next week when I have the proposal ready'. This means that the sales person says to the customer, 'Let's put something on our calendars to meet again and review my recommendation…how about next Friday at 10:00?'

Please understand how important this detail is. Too many sales are lost—or sales cycles extended unnecessarily—by not setting this specific calendar event for the proposal presentation. Once you leave the prospective customer's office, it becomes much more difficult to get something scheduled. Take advantage of being face-to-face, and schedule it before you leave. This habit alone will pay you huge dividends in terms of additional sales revenue and shortened sales cycles

The Steps of
The Customer Interview Phase

**1-
Introduction**

"I really appreciate the opportunity to meet, and to share some of the things we're doing with our customers.

Right up front I'll tell you that we aren't always able to help everyone ...

but I'll try to give you all of the information you need so that at the end of our meeting, you can decide where we go from there.

Before we get started, would it make sense if I told you a little more about what we do?"

Followed up by the sales person's brief commercial.

**2-
Build
Personal
Rapport**

"I'm curious, how long have you been at XYZ Company?"

Followed up by additional questions that are focused on the prospective customer as an individual.

**3-
Gather
Business
Information**

"I was wondering ... What experiences have you had with *insert sales person's type of company* in the past?"

Followed up by some discussion of the prospective customer's experiences.

"So based on all of those experiences, what kinds of things are you doing now to *insert service or product the sales person's company provides*?"

Followed up by some discussion about the prospective customer's current situation.

"In the past, when you've brought in new *insert sales person's type of company*, I'm curious ... what were some of the reasons?"

**4-
Close for
the Next
Calendar
Event**

"I really appreciate all of the time you've spent with me. When we first started talking, I told you that you'd be the one to decide where we go from here.

I can tell you that I do have some ideas, based on the information you've given me. And I'd like to show them to you. Does that make sense?"

The Customer Interview Phase
is the most important part of the sales process

In this phase, the Master Sales Person is getting the answers to the following critically important questions:

- How is the prospective customer currently doing what the master sales person offers?

- What results is the prospective customer getting from their current method?

- What reasons would the prospective customer have to change what they are currently doing?

The master sales person knows that these are the critical questions that need to be answered in every sales opportunity. He or she also knows that these questions must be asked at the right time in the process, and in the right way.

The transition questions in the diagram on page 124 are designed to move the sales person through an effective Customer Interview.

CHAPTER 5

THE 3RD PHASE OF SELLING: PRESENTING THE RECOMMENDATION

The third and final Phase of the 3-Phase sales process is Presenting the Recommendation. It still amazes me that so many people think that the sales person's main job is to present the sales proposal. There is a perception that the act of selling is synonymous with the act of telling someone how great your product or service is, and then showing them how much you know about it.

As you know from reading this far, or from your own practical experience, this is far from the truth. The Master Sales Person's job is almost completed by the time he or she gets to this point. The selling is really done during the Customer Interview Phase. That is where the Master Sales Person has built rapport with the prospective customer—remember the saying that people buy from people they like. And that is also where the Master Sales Person has gathered all of the key pieces of information so that his or her recommendation can be tailored specifically for that prospective customer—this is critical because a one-size-fits-all approach will not lead to sales success.

A WORD ABOUT PRICING AND FINANCIAL INFORMATION

Some situations and industries call for written proposals. If this is the case for your industry, please ensure that you keep all of the pricing information separate from the remainder of your proposal. There is a very practical reason for doing this.

There is a certain flow to Presenting the Recommendation that you will want to follow so that you maintain control of how the information is disclosed. If you include a pricing page in your proposal, and you provide this proposal document to your prospective customer to start the meeting, many times he or she will flip to the pricing page immediately.

When this happens, you have lost control of the meeting. Once a prospective customer sees pricing information, it is very difficult to get them thinking about anything other than pricing. Sometimes the prospective customer starts into a price negotiation at this point, and the sales person hasn't even had a chance to talk about key elements of the proposal yet. This is simply human nature.

The approach I use, instead, is to provide information throughout the meeting, piece by piece, so that the prospective customer is seeing only what I am talking about at that point in time. This way, I control the flow of the meeting.

What should you do if your prospective customer asks to see the pricing at the beginning of the meeting, or even during the meeting? This will happen sometimes, and the way I handle it is as follows:

PC   "Can we take a look at the pricing up front?"

SP   "I know that's a very important

part of your decision. And because of that, I have an entire section of my presentation dedicated specifically to pricing.

But some of the details in the pricing section may vary, depending on whether I have everything else correct in the rest of my proposal.

If you don't mind, let me make sure I have all of your requirements correct, and then we can spend as much time on pricing as you like."

I have never had a situation where this didn't work. My prospective customers have always respected the logic of this request, because it is put in terms of the benefit to them. They understand that I want to make sure I understand *their* requirements, so that the pricing I present makes sense for *them*.

When I train sales people to execute the Presenting the Recommendation Phase, I like to use a '4-page' approach. Each page of the recommendation represents a section of the presentation. In some cases, a sales person may need to vary from this somewhat, such as using more than one page in a particular section because of the volume of the information. But the idea is to think about Presenting the Recommendation in four distinct sections, or pages.

PRESENTING THE RECOMMENDATION:
PAGE 1 — REVIEW THE CUSTOMER OBJECTIVES

At the beginning of the meeting, I like to use the following introduction:

SP   "I'm really looking forward to showing you some of my ideas. Before I get to the details of my recommendation, though, I'd like to review what I understand to be

> your objectives, just to be sure I
> have a good understanding of
> what you're trying to accomplish.
>
> Does that make sense?"

As I'm saying this, I am handing the prospective customer a sheet of paper that has a list of what I understand their objectives to be. I like to use a bullet point list. And I use the exact points that we discussed during the Customer Interview Phase. Now you can see the value of the time you spent interviewing the prospective customer. You can take your notes from that meeting, and use the specific points—even using the prospective customer's own words and phrases—to indicate to him or her that you were listening and that you understand what they are trying to accomplish.

The document should look something like this:

Review of XYZ Company Objectives

- Objective #1
  - Additional notes and comments about Objective #1

- Objective #2
  - Additional notes and comments about Objective #2

- Objective #3
  - Additional notes and comments about Objective #3

- Etc.

Again, try to use as many of the prospective customer's own words as you can in the "Additional Notes and comments" section for each objective.

This document should be used to frame the first part of the meeting. There are two things the sales person is accomplishing by doing this. The first is obvious. The sales person is ensuring that nothing has changed, and that nothing has been missed.

The second thing the sales person is accomplishing, however, is somewhat less obvious. By starting the meeting with a review of the prospective customer's objectives, as opposed to starting right into the proposal, the Master Sales Person is continuing to implement Supportive Selling. He or she is always putting the interests of the prospective customer first.

When the sales person leads with the prospective customer's objectives, that prospective customer hears the message, 'I want to help you'. Conversely, when the sales person leads with the proposed products and services, the prospective customer hears the message, 'I want to sell you something'. Supportive Selling is all about helping and serving the prospective customer.

The wrap-up question after page 1 has been discussed is as follows:

SP   "Have I covered all of your
       objectives? Or have I missed
       anything, or gotten anything
       wrong?"

The sales person must—absolutely *must*—ask this question and get an answer from the prospective customer that the list of objectives is complete and accurate. Otherwise, there is no point in moving forward. Remember, the recommendation was put together based on this list of objectives. So if the list is incomplete or incorrect, moving forward would be a mistake.

It makes much more sense, in the case that the customer says that the list of objectives is incomplete or incorrect, to go back into the Customer Interview Phase and re-question the prospective customer. This will happen sometimes. And this is not a bad thing. Sometimes situations change, and the Master Sales Person needs to re-interview the prospective customer for new objectives. It is much better to do this than to plow forward with a proposal that no longer matches the prospective customer's objectives.

Once the sales person gets the answer that Page 1 is an accurate representation of the prospective customer's objectives, he or she can move forward to Page 2.

PRESENTING THE RECOMMENDATION:
PAGE 2 — THE RECOMMENDED SOLUTION

At this point in the meeting, the sales person has confirmed that he or she understands the objectives of the prospective customer. I like to use the following transition statement:

SP   "We have some recommendations for you that I'd like to review. And I'll show you how they tie back to your objectives.

      Does that make sense?"

As I'm saying this, I am handing the prospective customer a second sheet of paper that outlines my recommended solution. (The term 'solution' is used here to indicate any product, service or combination of products and/or services that you or your company provides for your customers.)

The document should look something like this:

Recommendation for XYZ Company

• Section 1: Description of Recommendation
- Overview or brief description of the solution (products & services) that are being recommended.

• Section 2: Solution Benefits
- Review of how this solution satisfies each of the prospective customer's objectives.

Notice what is, and what is not, included on Page 2. What is included is an explanation of the proposed solution, and a specific tie-back to each of the prospective customer's objectives. These sections can be in a bullet format, or a short paragraph. The sales person should use the format that will be most comfortable to present to the prospective customer. There should be just enough information to provide a good understanding of what the sales person is proposing, and how it ***specifically*** addresses each objective. Any appropriate product literature or other materials that reinforce the description of the solution, or the benefits, can also be used as backup.

What has not been included yet are two things: 1-Pricing, and 2-Timing of Purchase (or Schedule of Implementation.) These will be discussed separately—on their own pages. At this point, the sales person wants the entire spotlight to shine on the solution, and how it satisfies the prospective customer's objectives.

Earlier in this book, I mentioned that the Customer Interview was a time for the sales person to listen, but that the time for him or her to talk would come. Well, this is that time. This is the point at which the sales person gets to do most of the talking. But it is also important to ask questions as the solution is presented, such as, "Does that make sense?", or, "How does that sound?" This ensures that the customer is engaged, and that he or she understands what you are presenting.

The wrap-up question for Page 2 is similar to the wrap-up for Page 1:

SP "Before I move on to some of the other details, does what I've recommended make sense? Have I covered each of your objectives, and shown you how this recommendation will help you get there?"

Once again, the sales person must— absolutely *must*—ask this question and get an affirmative answer from the prospective customer before moving forward. If the prospective customer is not confident that his or her objectives are being met with the recommendation, then the sales person must resolve this issue prior to moving forward. What point is there to presenting pricing for a solution that won't satisfy the prospective customer's needs?

By the way, the prospective customer may mention price at this point. Let's say he or she says something like, "I can't really say whether it meets my needs or not, until I see the price." The way to handle this is to say, "I'm glad you brought that up, because we're just about to get to that. Other than the price, which we'll talk about in a minute, does it look like what I'm recommending makes sense?"

Remember, at this point the sales person is shining the spotlight on the proposed solution, to confirm that it will meet the prospective customer's objectives. If the solution is not doing that, then it needs to be reworked and re-presented at a future time. Price will not matter if the sales person is not presenting the right solution.

PRESENTING THE RECOMMENDATION:
PAGE 3 — THE IMPLEMENTATION SCHEDULE

At this point in the meeting, the sales person has confirmed that he or she understands the objectives of the prospective customer, and the prospective customer has agreed that the recommended solution meets those objectives.

You may not need a Page 3 for your recommendation. Page 3 is very useful for industries where the solution will be implemented in phases. If your industry is characterized by a single purchase date—such as buying a piece of equipment—then Page 3 may not be necessary.

If, on the other hand, your industry is characterized by implementation phases—such as long-term consulting engagements, software development, or construction projects, for example—then Page 3 is very useful. It is really an outline of the specific steps that need to be taken subsequent to this meeting.

Because I often recommend a phased approach with my consulting and training services, I like to use the following transition statement:

> SP   "Let's talk about what needs to happen to get things in place to meet your timeframe requirements, as I understand them."

As I'm saying this, I am handing the prospective customer a third sheet of paper that outlines my recommended schedule.

The document should look something like this:

XYZ Company Implementation Schedule		
	Action Description	Date
• Action 1	_____	dd/mm/yy
• Action 2	_____	dd/mm/yy
• Action 3	_____	dd/mm/yy
• Etc.		

PRESENTING THE RECOMMENDATION: PAGE 4 — THE FINANCIAL SUMMARY

At this point, the only thing left to cover is the pricing. If you have used a Page 3, you may have covered some pricing in that step of the discussion. This is often the case in my business, when I'm presenting training or consulting programs that have several phases. If pricing comes up during the Page 3 presentation, that is fine.

Remember that one of the most important things the Master Sales Person avoids doing is talking about price during the discussion of Page 1-Review the Customer Objectives— and Page 2-The Recommended Solution. During those discussions, particularly, the sales person wants to ensure that the spotlight is on the prospective customer's objectives, and on how the sales person's recommendation will satisfy those objectives.

I like to use the following transition statement to lead into the discussion of pricing and the financial summary:

> SP   "The final thing we need to cover
>   is the financial summary."

As I'm saying this, I am handing the prospective customer a fourth sheet of paper that outlines the pricing, and any other financially related points that I would like to cover.

The document should look something like this:

XYZ Company Financial Summary

- **Section 1: Investment Summary**
  - Overview of the financial investment (i.e. price) that the prospective customer will make to acquire the solution.

- **Section 2: Return-on-Investment (ROI)**
  - This is an optional section. If the sales person can present specific financial benefits of implementing this solution, they should be explained here, so that they offset the out-of-pocket expenditures that will be required in the Investment Summary.

UH OH—NOW I HAVE TO CLOSE THE DEAL!

And now comes that moment of truth that too many inexperienced and seasoned sales people fear—the dreaded close! I am being facetious about this because I believe that the closing process is the second most misunderstood aspect of professional selling. It ranks right behind the misconception that selling is all about presenting, as opposed to asking questions and listening.

There are entire books written about closing techniques. And who among us has not heard a sales person described as a 'closer'? Well, I am going to bust that myth into pieces. There is no such thing as a good closer, unless that person is also executing the remainder of the sales steps effectively.

Sales people may have been able to get away with that hard closing style in the past, but today's prospective customers are much more informed and experienced. They will not fall for that approach—nor should they.

When closing is done correctly, it is a logical, natural and comfortable follow-on to the sales discussion. The truth of closing is that the Master Sales Person is closing throughout the entire sales process! That's right. Every time I suggested that the sales person needed to gain agreement from the prospective customer before moving to the next step—whether during the Prospecting, Customer Interview or the Presenting the Recommendation Phase—that small agreement was a close.

Closing a sale is not some heavy-handed and abrasive technique that the sales person uses to put the prospective customer under so much pressure that they have to say 'Yes'. Who wants to do that for a living? I sure don't.

Think about it this way. The Master Sales Person spreads the close out across the entire sales process. This way, each close is simply a small agreement to move forward through the process a little bit at a time. This is very easy and comfortable for both the sales person and the prospective customer to do.

The opposite approach is for the sales person to move into presentation-mode too early in the process—before he or she has established rapport and really has an understanding of what the prospective customer's objectives are. When this happens, the sales person is boxed in. Because he or she hasn't moved through the proper steps, all of those opportunities to gain small agreements and to make small closes along the way have been sacrificed. The only option at this point is to go for a hard close.

And that's where the trouble starts with sales. Neither the sales person nor the prospective customer likes that process. Think about how this may have happened to you when you've purchased a car. I am not saying that all auto dealers sell this way—some have actually evolved quite admirably into a Supportive Selling style. But too many are still oriented toward the quick sell, high pressure close.

The following statement is a very good and acceptable 'closing phrase', after you and your prospective customer have moved through the four Pages of Presenting the Recommendation. It is one of my favorites:

> SP   "I really appreciate the time you've spent with me, and I'm looking forward to working with you!"

As I say this, I look at the customer and I reach out to shake his or her hand. This is all there is to a good close. There is no need to go through the gyrations of a Ben Franklin T-chart close, or a hand-the-pen-across-the-table with a pre-completed contract close, or any number of other cheesy and, quite frankly, insulting closing moves. Simply make a nice warm statement—from one professional to another—that you are looking forward to working with your prospective customer.

You have now converted the prospective customer to an actual customer— congratulations! You started with the raw material of a potential customer. You converted them from a potential customer into a prospective customer when they agreed to sit down with you and engage in a 1-to-1 discussion. And you converted them from a prospective customer into an actual customer after moving *with them*—not doing something *to them*—through the three Phases of the Supportive Selling process.

But your work is not done. The good news is that neither is your opportunity. While the sales person has completed the sales process—the prospective customer has moved through the sales funnel and exited the narrow end at the bottom as an actual customer—there is a post-sale step that needs to be completed.

Presenting the Recommendation
The Four Pages of a Good Proposal

PAGE 1:
Review the Prospective Customer's
Objectives

PAGE 2:
Explain the Recommended Solution

PAGE 3:
Review the Implementation Schedule
or Purchase Timeframe

PAGE 4:
Present the Pricing and Financial
Summary

The final phase of
The Supportive Selling Process is
Presenting the Recommendation

During this phase, the Master Sales Person ensures that there are four distinct steps in the discussion and the presentation of material.

The objectives of each Page of the recommendation are as follows:

- Page 1 – Ensure that the objectives are complete and accurate; Show the prospective customer that the sales person has been listening;

- Page 2 – Show the prospective customer how the recommended solution will address each objective;

- Page 3 – Create forward momentum by outlining the next steps for the prospective customer to take;

- Page 4 – Keep the price as the last item to discuss (price negotiation too early in the process will derail the Presenting the Recommendation Phase.)

CHAPTER 6

THE POST SALE:
DELIVERY
&
SERVICE

There are two aspects to Delivery & Service that need to be discussed, and to which the Master Sales Person needs to devote attention: Responsibility and Opportunity.

THE SALES PERSON'S RESPONSIBILITY

Each industry, and even different companies within the same industry, are set up to handle this aspect differently. On the one end of the spectrum, there are companies that do not expect their sales people to do anything other than sell—period. Once the prospective customer becomes an actual customer, the sales person's job is to move on and find more customers.

At the other end of the spectrum, there are companies that are organized in a way that each sales person also carries ongoing customer service responsibility for the entire customer relationship into the future. In these companies, sales people are also customer service representatives.

Most companies are somewhere in between these two extremes. While the sales person does not carry total responsibility for delivering what is sold, and for servicing the relationship, he or she is certainly involved to some degree in managing this relationship.

So, as a general rule, what should the sales person's involvement and responsibility be in this post-sales step? In my experience, the sales person should always offer himself or herself to the customer as the key point of contact—unless this is specifically contrary to their company's policy for some reason.

Even if the sales person does not have formal responsibility for Delivery & Service, there is tremendous value in being that up-front person for the customer. Sometimes all this means is being the 'traffic cop' so that the customer knows that he or she always has a place to go if there is an issue—and that the sales person will take responsibility for directing the issue to the proper person, and will stay with the issue until it is resolved.

Taking this extra responsibility certainly shows professionalism to the customer. But more importantly, it continues to demonstrate the basic philosophy of Supportive Selling throughout the entire relationship. It validates that the sales person has a true interest in the customer's success—and that this interest is genuine. It lasts beyond just closing the deal and cashing the commission check.

THE FIRST RELATIONSHIP OPPORTUNITY: CROSS-SELLING

It's not all just about responsibility. There are also other important reasons for the sales person to remain engaged throughout Delivery & Service.

If your business has any degree of cross-selling opportunity, then the relationship you create with your customer is financially valuable to your future. The term 'cross-sell' simply means selling additional products or services to existing customer. Cross-selling can be thought of as repeat selling, and growing your customer relationship.

Consider two scenarios. In Scenario 1, the sales person has made a sale. He then contacts the customer six months later—and this is the first time he has called to check in—and he proceeds to tell the customer that his company has a new product or service that he would like to stop by and talk about.

In Scenario 2, the sales person has made a sale, but in this case she has made a point of stopping in or calling every few weeks, just to make sure that everything was going well with the product she sold. Six months later, on one of her stop-by visits, she mentions to her contact that her company has developed a new product or service, and that it may be something they can talk about over lunch on Monday.

Which sales person is better positioned to capitalize on the cross-sell opportunity? The answer is clear. The sales person in Scenario 2 is much more likely to make the additional sale.

There is another dynamic that is relevant to this discussion. Much research has been done on the topic of the differential between the cost and effort to cross-sell to an existing customer versus the cost and effort necessary to acquire a new customer. While the specific numerical findings of the studies vary somewhat, the dynamics of the conclusion are always the same: It is much more expensive and time consuming—usually by a factor of between five to ten times—to acquire a new customer than it is to close the same sized sale with an existing customer.

By the way, this is not intended to suggest in any way that acquiring new customers is not important—it is *critically* important. Marketing and prospecting for new customers is absolutely necessary for the health of any business. The point being emphasized here is that there must be a balance between acquiring new customers, and taking care of existing customers so that they will continue to buy.

THE SECOND RELATIONSHIP
OPPORTUNITY: REFERRALS

The second reason that a Master Sales Person focuses on Delivery & Service is referrals. This is another area of business that has been widely studied. As I have already mentioned, it has been determined that when customers are dissatisfied with a product or service, they will tell many more people than if they are satisfied.

For this reason, the sales person needs to ensure his or her customer's satisfaction just for defensive reasons. If a customer reaches a point of dissatisfaction with a purchase, it is very advantageous to the sales person to know this early—when he or she can do something about it—rather than after the fact, when it is too late.

I have seen and experienced many situations where an episode of customer dissatisfaction has strengthened the relationship because the sales person was able to handle the issue, and in so doing was able to demonstrate a high level of care for the customer. This level of care actually created a competitive advantage out of what was initially a negative situation, because it strengthened the bond between the sales person and the customer. Once again, the principles of Supportive Selling are in play when the sales person is helping the customer to deal with a problem by providing service.

There is not a business where problems do not occur. I can state with 100% certainty that there is not one business on this planet where things go right every single time. There will be issues—there will be dissatisfied customers. Knowing this to be the case, the Master Sales Person actually takes *advantage* of these situations by becoming aware of them early, and taking ownership for them through the point of resolution.

Let's take another look at our earlier scenarios. The sales person from Scenario 1, after not calling his customer for six months, calls him and asks him who he knows who might be a good referral for him. To add another degree of challenge to his referral request, imagine that the customer has not been totally happy with the purchase for several months, and this is the first time the sales person is learning about it.

Conversely, the sales person in Scenario 2, who has been building a steady relationship with her customer, does the same thing—she calls her customer for referrals. It is actually quite likely that she probably wouldn't even have to ask for referrals, because in this scenario the customer would have had numerous opportunities to give them to her during one of their many conversations. And if there had been a problem with her product or service, she would have known about it very early, and would have been able to address it.

CLOSE THE SALE—OPEN THE RELATIONSHIP

When it comes to Delivery & Service, the Master Sales Person realizes that cross-sales and referrals are excellent ways to reload the sales funnel. And the more satisfied customers the Master Sales Person is able to develop, the less effort it takes to load the funnel.

The next time you close a sale, don't focus on the word 'close'. This is a very limiting word, and one that is used too much in sales. 'Closing' sounds like something you do *to* a person, and it implies finality in the sales process—kind of like leaving a room and closing a door. Instead, what the Master Sales Person is really doing is opening, not closing. He or she is opening a personal and business relationship where there is mutual *support* between two parties—and the sale is just a benefit that comes from that relationship.

THE CONCLUSION...
AND THE BEGINNING

The conclusion to this book is also meant to be a beginning for the reader. No matter where you are in your journey—whether you have never sold professionally or whether you have been selling professionally for many years—an important key to success is ongoing learning.

Take some concepts from this book that appeal to you, and begin implementing them immediately. Just by doing one little thing differently on a consistent basis, you can make major changes in the results you get.

Please visit me at:

www.sellingpointsgroup.com or email me at **pbruening@sellingpointsgroup.com**. I'd like to know how you're doing. And let me know if I can provide you with some ideas concerning a sales challenge you're dealing with. I wish you good selling, and the best of luck!

ABOUT THE AUTHOR

Peter K. Bruening is an author, professional speaker and sales & leadership training consultant. He spends his days helping business professionals learn effective sales and leadership techniques, and working with them to implement these skills in their careers. Peter Bruening founded The SellingPoints Group, Inc. (SPGi) in early 2004 after more than two decades of successful sales & management experience. Peter earned his MBA from The University of Pittsburgh-Katz School of Business in 1984.